ALAN WATTS

I0163272

ETERNALLY NOW

QUOTES FOR KIDS!

Copyright © 2024 by Eternally Now Publishing

Written by Alan Watts and Steve Brewer

All rights reserved. No part of this publication may be reproduced, distributed or transmitted in any form or by any means, including photocopying, recording, or other electronic or mechanical methods, without the prior written permission of the publisher, except in the case of brief quotations embodied in critical reviews and certain other noncommercial uses permitted by copyright law. For permission requests, write to orders@eternallynowpublishing.com

The intent of the author is only to offer information of a general nature. The author assumes no responsibility for actions taken based on the information in this book.

ISBN: 979-8-218-56251-9

First edition, 2024.

Find out more at: www.eternallynowpublishing.com

To the parent or kid who turns these pages and has chosen higher awareness as the path to mental fortitude.
Always remember, thoughts and beliefs co-create the reality we live in.
The moment is what we have, make the most of it!

"You can't live at all unless you can live fully now. "

Living fully now means experiencing each moment, without judgement or attachment. This mindset allows us to embrace the present moment and let go of past regrets and future anxieties. This simple yet profound statement reminds us that we are often wasting valuable time dwelling on the past or worrying about the future.

"This very moment, this very world, this very body is the point. Now. You see? But, if you're seeking something beyond all the time, you never get with it. You're never here."

The truth is that we are constantly chasing after things that will never truly fulfill us. By focusing on the present moment, we can achieve a sense of inner peace, happiness, and connection with something greater than ourselves. When we truly embrace the here and now, we can experience the beauty of life and the countless opportunities that present themselves each moment.

"When we dance, the journey itself is the point, as when we play music the playing itself is the point. And exactly the same thing is true in meditation. Meditation is the discovery that the point of life is always arrived at in the immediate moment."

In dancing, we don't just wait for the song to end.
Meditation isn't about reaching enlightenment.
It's about being present in each moment.
The joy isn't in the goal, it's in the growth.
When we embrace the journey, the journey becomes our reward. Life is not a problem to be solved, it's a reality to be experienced.

"Real travel requires a maximum of unscheduled wandering, for there is no other way of discovering surprises and marvels, which, as I see it, is the only good reason for not staying at home."

Every journey has the potential to unveil marvels, but only if we are willing to step off the beaten path. Let curiosity guide you and see where it takes you. After all, the essence of travel lies not just in the destinations, but in the delightful surprises along the way. In the end, these moments are the true treasures that remind us why we venture beyond our comfort zones.

"To have faith is to trust
yourself to the water.
When you swim you don't grab hold
of the water, because if you do
you will sink and drown.
Instead you relax, and float."

This quote is a powerful reminder
that faith and trust are not about holding
on tightly, but rather about letting go
and allowing ourselves to be supported
by something greater. It's about
trusting in the process and having
faith in ourselves and the
world around us.

"When we attempt to exercise power or control over someone else, we cannot avoid giving that person the very same power or control over us."

This concept is all about the universal law of cause and effect, which states that for every action, there is an equal and opposite reaction. In other words, if we try to control or manipulate someone, we're essentially giving them the power to control or manipulate us. It's a powerful reminder that we should always treat others with respect and empathy, because we never know when the roles might reverse.

"Man has to realize that he is an integral part of nature...
He is just as much a natural form as a seagull or a mountain. And if he doesn't realize that, he uses his technical powers to destroy his environment... to foul his own nest."

We often perceive the world around us as a set of distinct objects, each with its specific value. However, nature's interconnectedness is evident in the way we depend on one another for survival. This interdependence highlights the importance of respecting the environment and maintaining and sense of unity. It's crucial to recognize the long-term consequences of your actions, as they can have ripple effects that reach beyond our current concerns.

"Before you were born there was
this same nothing-at-all forever.
And yet... you happened.
And if you happened once,
you can happen again."

Life after death refers to the belief
that one will die and be reborn in another
being based on their previous lives.
This interpretation should encourage people
to do good and help others because their
virtues will spread positive energy.

"People who exude love are apt to give things away. They are in every way like rivers; they stream. And so when they collect possessions and things they like, they are apt to give them to other people. Because, have you ever noticed that when you start giving things away, you keep getting more?"

This behavior stems from a deep seeded belief that happiness multiplies when shared. Have you ever noticed how a kind gesture can brighten someone's day? Those who embody love understand the value of connection over material things.

"We do not "come into" this world; we come out of it, as leaves from a tree. As the ocean "waves," the universe "peoples." Every individual is an expression of the whole realm of nature, a unique action of the total universe."

Did you know that we don't "come into" this world, but rather, we "come out" of it? It's like leaves on a tree - they don't come from the tree, but rather, they're a part of it. In the same way, we're not separate from the universe, but rather, we're a unique expression of it. Every individual is a part of the whole realm of nature, a unique action of the total universe.

"You are in relationships with the external world that are, on the whole, incredibly harmonious. But we have this rather myopic way of looking at things. And we screen out from attention anything that is not immediately important to a scanning system based on sensing danger."

We tend to focus immediate attention on threats and challenges, neglecting the broader perspectives that tie us to the environment. By doing so, we inadvertently create barriers that hinder our understanding and appreciation of the interconnectedness that exists between us and the world we live in.

"Let's ask, 'How big is the sun?'
Are we going to define the sun as
limited by the extent of its fire?
That's one possible definition.
But we could equally well define
the sphere of the sun by the
extent of its light."

You could try to define how big the
sun is by the extent of its fire.
Although, its rather difficult to keep
track of the extent of its light because we're
inside it. Therefore we have arbitrarily
agreed to define the sun by the limit of its
visible fire. But you see, in reality,
there are no separate events.

"When you look out of your eyes, at nature happening out there, you're looking at you. That's the real you. The you that goes on of itself."

When we look out of our eyes, at the natural world unfolding around us, we're not just witnessing the beauty and complexity of life, but also ourselves. This real authentic "me" is the part that goes on of itself unfiltered by society or culture. This intimate glimpse into the real you reveals the raw, untamed spirit that resides within each of us.

"This is the real secret of life...
to be completely engaged with
what you are doing in the here
and now - and instead of calling
it work, realize it is play."

You're supposed to work to earn enough
money, to give you sufficient leisure time
for something entirely different called
'having fun', or 'playing'. And this is the
most ridiculous division of things because
everything that we do, however tough it is,
however strenuous, can be turned into play.
So the point is, therefore, that you can do
everything you have to do in this spirit.

"And if you stay in your mind all the time, you are over-rational. In other words, you're like a very rigid bridge which because it has got no give, no craziness in it, is going to be blown down in the first hurricane."

When we stay in our minds all the time, we become over-rational, lacking the flexibility to adapt and enjoy life's small pleasures. This rigidity can lead us to become susceptible to setbacks and disappointments. By embracing the bouncy, spontaneous nature of life, we can withstand any storm and emerge stronger. So, the next time you're feeling overwhelmed, embrace the craziness.

"Through our eyes, the universe is perceiving itself. Through our ears, the universe is listening to its harmonies. We are the witnesses through which the universe becomes conscious of its glory, of its magnificence."

Imagine that, every time we open our eyes, the universe is experiencing itself through our perception. And when we listen to the world around us, we're giving the universe the chance to hear its own melodies. We're the mirrors that reflect the universe's beauty back to itself, making it aware of its own grandeur.

"Light is a relationship between electrical energy and eyeballs. It is you, in other words, who evoke the world and you evoke the world in accordance with what kind of a 'you' you are."

Light is the manifestation of electrical energy interacting with the eyeballs, creating the world we see around us. Each person possesses a unique perspective on the world, determined by the characteristics of the emotions they convey. In essence, light is you, and you are the author of the world you create through your eyes.

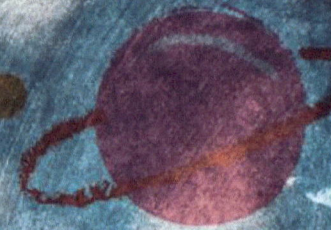

"Really, the fundamental, ultimate mystery -- the only thing you need to know to understand the deepest metaphysical secrets -- is this: that for every outside there is an inside and for every inside there is an outside, and although they are different, they go together."

This idea is an underlying truth that can help us understand the universe and our place in it. It's a reminder that everything we see and experience is part of a larger whole and that every aspect of the universe is interconnected.

www.ingramcontent.com/pod-product-compliance
Lightning Source LLC
Chambersburg PA
CBHW042102040426

42448CB00002B/103